HORN TOOTING

An Examination

I0737558

HORN TOOTING

An Examination

Written by M. Thomas
Illustrated by Femke de Jong

RP MINIS
PHILADELPHIA

Copyright © 2025 by Running Press
Illustrations copyright © 2025 by Femke de Jong
Cover copyright © 2025 by Hachette Book Group, Inc.

Hachette Book Group supports the right to free expression and the value of copyright. The purpose of copyright is to encourage writers and artists to produce the creative works that enrich our culture.

The scanning, uploading, and distribution of this book without permission is a theft of the author's intellectual property. If you would like permission to use material from the book (other than for review purposes), please contact permissions@hbgusa.com. Thank you for your support of the author's rights.

RP Minis®
Hachette Book Group
1290 Avenue of the Americas, New York, NY 10104
www.runningpress.com
@Running_Press

First Edition: September 2025

Published by RP Minis, an imprint of Hachette Book Group, Inc. The RP Minis name and logo is a registered trademark of Hachette Book Group, Inc.

Contact specialmarkets@hbgusa.com regarding special discounts for bulk purchases.

The publisher is not responsible for websites (or their content) that are not owned by the publisher.

Design by Sara Puppala

ISBN: 979-8-89414-093-3

Made in Dongguan, China (HKD) 06/25 #01

Contents

Prelude: An Introduction
5

Provenance:
Origins of an Idiom
9

Parallels:
Equivalents in Other Languages
21

Parting: A Farewell
31

Prelude: An Introduction

"Not to toot my own horn, but . . ."

These words have preceded many a boast, brag, *humble*brag, and self-aggrandizement. But what exactly is the significance of this evocative phrase?

In this petite volume, we'll explore the history of own-horn tooting, as well as its international counterparts. Hopefully, you'll learn a thing or two—and then you can celebrate that newfound knowledge with a toot of your very own horn!

PROVENANCE: ORIGINS OF AN IDIOM

To "toot your own horn"—or, in some regions and during some time periods, "blow your own horn" or "blow your own trumpet"—is an idiom that means to brag about your own accomplishments, possibly excessively so.

As with many expressions, this one has evolved over time, waxing and waning in usage, and its exact inventor is impossible to identify. But there are several theories and pieces of evidence to help us tell the story of this turn of phrase.

One common theory is that the expression comes from the age-old practice of blowing a trumpet or a horn to announce the arrival of a prominent figure, such as a royal or an important guest. Some today would consider figuratively doing so for oneself to be egotistical. Others might call it confident!

A very early usage of a similar construction to the modern saying is biblical—Matthew verse 6:2, written in the first century, reads (in the King James Version), "Therefore when thou doest thine alms, do not sound a trumpet before thee, as the hypocrites do in the synagogues and in the streets, that they may have glory of men." The message is clear: these teachings fall on the side of *not* tooting one's own horn.

Other delightfully old-timey examples followed, not all of them in favor of the humble approach.

In 1509, the Dutch theologian and philosopher Erasmus of Rotterdam wrote an essay called *Stultitiae Laus*, or *In Praise of Folly*. Sir Thomas Chaloner's 1549 translation of the text included the line: "And what (I praie you) maie be

more apt or better fittyng, than dame Foly to praise hir selfe, and be hir owne trumpet? for who can livelier descrive me, then I my selfe?" By 1668, in John Wilson's translation, this had become: "Nor do I esteem a rush that call it a foolish and insolent thing to praise one's self. Be it as foolish as they would make it, so they confess it proper: and what can be more than that Folly be her own trumpet? For who can set me out better than myself, unless perhaps I could be better known to another than to myself?" You tell 'em, Erasmus!

Early versions of the expression seem to have made their way into more common parlance by somewhere around the eighteenth century. The Warren-Adams letters, a grouping of missives exchanged between John Adams, Samuel Adams, and James Warren around the time of the American Revolution in the 1770s, included the line,

"I think modesty is highly overrated as a virtue—my motto is 'Toot your own horn lest the same never be tooted.'"

In the US, the version "toot your own horn" has since decisively overtaken any variant that includes the word *trumpet*, and the use of "toot" rather than "blow" conjures the mental image of a horn perhaps more similar to the one you'll find included with this book than to a modern trumpet.

Regardless of where exactly this phrase came from, we can be sure it will continue to evolve as our language does, adding a sprinkle of whimsy, delight, and (perhaps false) humility to any good-natured brag, possibly for centuries to come.

PARALLELS: EQUIVALENTS IN OTHER LANGUAGES

English speakers aren't the only ones who like to dress up self-praise in evocative idioms. Here are a few examples of similar expressions from around the world:

Chinese

吹牛 *(Chuīniú)*

Inflate a cow

Danish

Pudse din egen glorie

Polish your own halo

Ananas i egen juice

Pineapple in its own juice

Dutch

Jezelf een schouderklopje geven
Give yourself a pat on the back

Jezelf op de borst slaan
Beat yourself on the chest

Estonian

Kes koera saba kergitab,
kui koer ise?
Who wags the dog's tail if
not the dog himself?

Finnish

Kukas se kissan hännän nostaa ellei kissa itse?

Who lifts the cat's tail if not the cat itself?

Tehdä itsestään numero

Make yourself a number

French

S'envoyer des fleurs

To send yourself flowers

German

Sich selbst beweihräuchern

Perfume yourself with incense

Hungarian

Fényezni magam

Shine myself

Italian

Se la canta e se la suona

Sings it to himself and plays it to himself

Japanese

自画自賛 *(Jiga jisan)*

The painter praising his own painting

Latvian

Kas sunim asti cels, ja ne pats?

Who will lift the dog's tail
if not the dog himself?

Russian

Сам себя не похвалишь—
никто не похвалит

If you don't praise yourself,
no one will

Spanish

Tirarse flores

To throw yourself flowers

Parting: A Farewell

Hopefully this has been an illuminating journey through the surprising story of tooting one's own horn. Armed with your newfound knowledge, go forth and exalt your own achievements without shame!

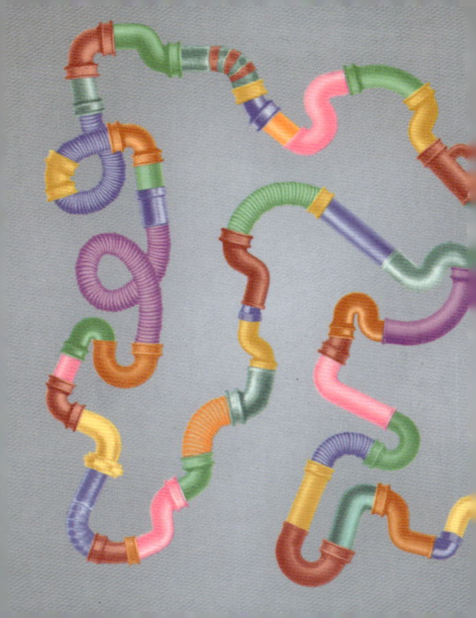